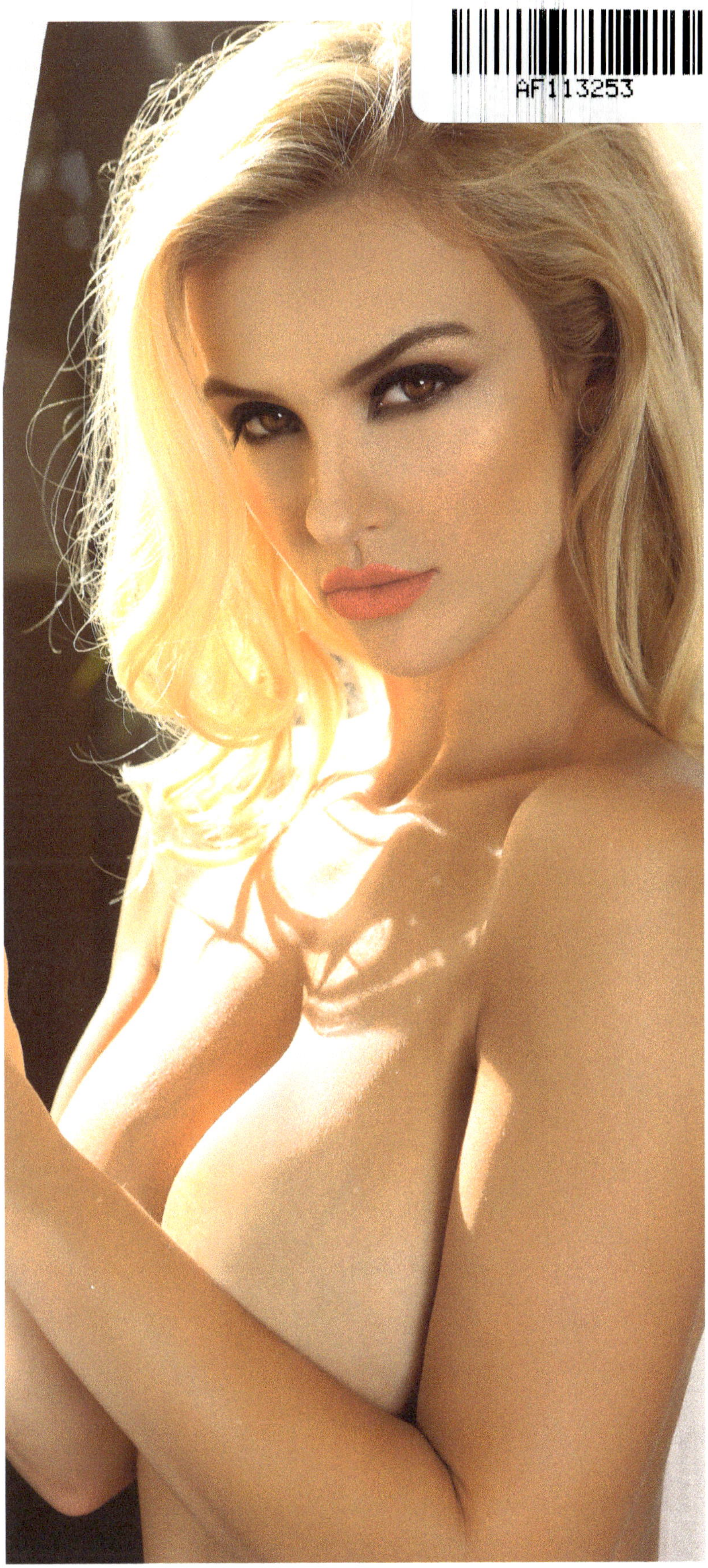

AF113253

Kandy

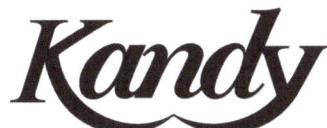

US PRINT SUBSCRIPTIONS ONLY
GET THIS ISSUE AS PART OF YOUR PRINT SUBSCRIPTION!

Mail to:
Kandy Enterprises
7260 W Azure Dr. Ste 140-639
Las Vegas, NV 89130

Yes! I want KANDY! SEND ME:

☐ **6 issues for $54(1 year)**
Suggested Newsstand $14.95 per issue

First Name

Last Name

Street Address

Street Address

City

State

Zip Code

Payment Must Be Enclosed
Please allow 6 to 8 weeks for delivery of first issue. **For Credit card and other payment options https://kandy.store**

EDITOR'S LETTER

This special edition features a few of the top glamour pictorials featured in Kandy.

Artificial Intelligence (AI) is conquering social media. Daily, there are more AI generated women. Pretty soon, your Instagram feed will be 99% AI-generated fake girls. As we witnessed this invasion, we decided to fight back. Our best weapon is the Kandy girls themselves. A few of the top glamour models who have appeared in Kandy magazine are here and a selection of images from their sizzling hot Kandy features.

There are Kandy girls on daybeds, balconies and on the rocks. There are Kandy girls surfside and bedside. There are Kandy girls pressed up against walls and windows. There are Kandy girls covered in bedsheets and hair – lots and lots of hair. There are Kandy girls with spearfishing guns. There are Kandy girls in stockings, bikini bottoms, thongs, sarongs, and nothing at all. There are blondes and brunettes. There are Kandy girls from Italy and the United Kingdom. There are Kandy girls from Seattle, San Francisco, and Sacramento.

Say hello to Kandy Magazine Glamour Girls Midsummer Sweets. And do not forget you get more Kandy in our mobile apps available in the Apple Appstore and Amazon Appstore. Digital editions are available on Zinio.com and Magzter.com.

Subscribe digitally at www.kandymag.com/digital and buy print subscriptions at www.kandy.store

- Shantal Monique @shantalmonique
- DJ Amie Rose
- Chloe Crawford @chloelcrawford
- Elisa de Panicis @elisadepanicis
- Brittany Danyelle @brittanydanyelle0
- Nina Carla @nina_carla
- Amanda Paris @missamandaparis

Cheers!

Ron Kuchler
Editor in Chief

**US PRINT SUBSCRIPTIONS ONLY
GET THIS ISSUE AS PART OF YOUR
PRINT SUBSCRIPTION!**

Mail to:
Kandy Enterprises
7260 W Azure Dr. Ste 140-639
Las Vegas, NV 89130

Yes! I want KANDY! SEND ME:

☐ **6 issues for $54 (1 year)**
Suggested Newsstand $14.95 per issue

_____
First Name

_____
Last Name

_____
Street Address

_____
Street Address

_____
City

_____
State

_____
Zip Code

Payment Must Be Enclosed
Please allow 6 to 8 weeks for delivery of
first issue. **For Credit card and other
payment options https://kandy.store**

Editor in Chief
Ron Kuchler

Managing Editor
David Packo

Associate Editor
Steve Scala

Director of Marketing
Bill Nychay

Cover Model
Shantal Monique

Contributing Photographers
Mike Prado, Karina Chancey, Aaron Riveroll,
Nova Prime PR, Jaime Morton Hawley

Contact Us
Kandy Enterprises LLC
7260 W Azure Dr. Ste 140-639
Las Vegas, NV 89130
www.kandymag.com
facebook @kandymagazine
twitter.com @kandy_magazine
instagram @kandymagazine

General Inquiries - info@kandymag.com
Letters to The Editor - letters@kandymag.com
Copyright - legal@kandymag.com
Subscription Inquiries - subscriptions@kandymag.com

© 2023 VOLUME 13 ISSUE 5
MIDSUMMER SWEETS
Kandy Enterprises LLC.
All Rights Reserved.

**US PRINT SUBSCRIPTIONS ONLY
GET THIS ISSUE AS PART OF YOUR
PRINT SUBSCRIPTION!**
Mail to:
Kandy Enterprises
7260 W Azure Dr. Ste 140-639
Las Vegas, NV 89130

Yes! I want KANDY! SEND ME:

☐ **6 issues for $54 (1 year)**
Suggested Newsstand $14.95 per issue

_____
First Name

_____
Last Name

_____
Street Address

_____
Street Address

_____
City

_____
State

_____
Zip Code

Payment Must Be Enclosed
Please allow 6 to 8 weeks for delivery of first issue. **For Credit card and other payment options https://kandy.store**

CHLOE CRAWFORD

A Magician Who Makes Her Top Disappear

Photos Jaime Morton Hawley
Courtesy Nova Prime PR

Photos: Jaime Morton Hawley @jaimemortonhawley
MUA: Edna Trogen @edna_trogen
Hair: Simona Barbato @simobarbato
Wardrobe: Plumeria Intimates @plumeriaswimwear
Location: Oia Sunset Villas - Santorini, Greece @oiasunsetvillas
Event: Destination Cover @destinationcover
PR: Nova Prime PR @novaprimepr

PROFESSION
Magician

KANDY WORD PLAY
What Chloe thinks when we say ..

Naked?
Swim

Sleep?
Over

iPhone?
Selfie

Man.. we should have followed with **"PILLOW"**

HOMETOWN
Portsmouth, England, UK

HERITAGE
British

KANDY WORD PLAY
What Chloe thinks when we say..

Luxury?
Yacht

Sex ?
Love

Yummy?
Candy

She can speak five languages
English, Spanish, Portuguese, French, and Italian.
Not just another pretty face, after all, is she?

SHANTAL Monique

Our Cover Model Is Hotter Than Your AI Girl

Photos Mike Prado
Hair and Makeup Jennifer Irene

HOMETOWN
Seattle, Washington

MEASUREMENTS
32-26-34

FAVORITE FLOWER
Tulips

DREAM DESTINATION
The Mediterranean

IG @SHANTALMONIQUE

Brittany Danyelle

A Trip Through Brittany's World

Photos Aaron Riveroll

NINA CARLA
Too Hot for Google Play 3X

TRUE STORY
Three times Nina was featured in Kandy and each time the Google Play censors removed our app after we published her photos. Shall we go for 4?

AMANDA PARIS
AMERICAN DREAMGIRL

Photos Mike Prado

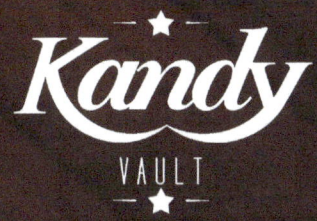

"I'm a R & B girl at heart

WHAT UP BIG SIS?!

I have 3 younger brothers

www.ingramcontent.com/pod-product-compliance
Lightning Source LLC
LaVergne TN
LVHW070524070526
838199LV00072B/6698